FOOD

POTATOES

Jillian Powell

WAYLAND

Titles in the series

BREAD   EGGS   FISH   FRUIT
MILK   PASTA   POTATOES
POULTRY   RICE   VEGETABLES

First published in 1996 by Wayland (Publishers) Ltd
61 Western Road, Hove, East Sussex, BN3 1JD, England

Series Editor: Sarah Doughty
Editor: Liz Harman
Design: Jean Wheeler
Illustration: Peter Bull
Cover: Zul Mukhida, Chapel Studios; photostylist Liz Miller

British Library Cataloguing in Publication Data
Powell, Jillian
Potatoes – (Food)
1. Potatoes – Juvenile literature
2. Cookery (Potatoes) – Juvenile literature
I. Title
641.3'521

ISBN 0 7502 1976 9

Typeset by Jean Wheeler

Printed and bound in Italy by L.E.G.O. S.p.A., Vicenza

Title page picture: Andean Indians selling potatoes at a market in Peru.

Picture acknowledgements

AKG 22 (bottom); Cephas 15 (top), 17 (top), 19 (top), 21 (top), 25 (top); Chapel Studios 4–5, 5 (bottom), 11 (top), 12 (top), 14 (left), 15 (bottom), 19 (bottom), 20 (bottom), 24 (both), 25 (bottom); Bruce Coleman 17 (bottom); James Davis Travel Photography 11 (bottom); Mary Evans 7 (both), 8, 9 (top), 23 (top); Eye Ubiquitous 14 (right), 16 (top); Life File 10 (top), 13 (bottom); Edward Parker title page, 6 (both), 22 (top); Potato Marketing Board contents page, 10 (bottom), 12 (bottom), 16 (bottom), 18 (both), 20 (top), 21 (bottom); Topham Picturepoint 4 (left), 9 (bottom), 13 (top); Visual Arts Library 23 (bottom).

Contents

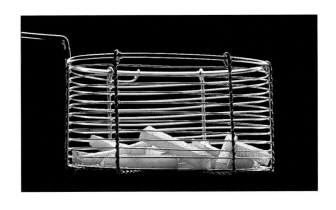

The popular potato

Potatoes are one of the world's most important food crops, grown in Europe, the USA, Australia, New Zealand, Russia, China and India. After wheat, rice and maize (corn), they are the world's fourth most widely grown crop.

◀ Potatoes first grew in the Andes Mountains of South America. People like these women in Bolivia have harvested potatoes by hand for hundreds of years.

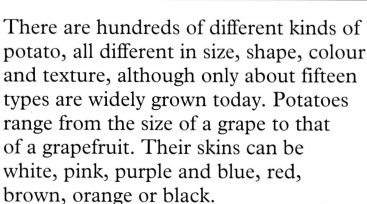

There are hundreds of different kinds of potato, all different in size, shape, colour and texture, although only about fifteen types are widely grown today. Potatoes range from the size of a grape to that of a grapefruit. Their skins can be white, pink, purple and blue, red, brown, orange or black.

Some potatoes are round and smooth, others are long and knobbly. Potatoes can be coloured inside, like the small, black Congo or the red Cardinal.

Potatoes grow quickly and easily and are a nutritious food for people and animals. They are grown on farms, smallholdings and in gardens.

Potatoes are a healthy food which can be cooked in many different ways and eaten with meat, poultry, fish, eggs, and vegetables.

◀ Potatoes can be served in many different ways. This boy is eating a potato waffle.

Every year, each person eats about 110 kg of potatoes in the UK, and about 52 kg in the USA. Over half of the potatoes eaten in the USA are in processed foods such as chips and crisps.

Potatoes in the past

Potatoes were being farmed in the Andes Mountains of Peru, South America, as long as 5,000 years ago. The people of the Inca civilization, which was at its height from about 1438–1532, found a way of keeping potatoes through the winter months. They left them out on frosty nights to soften them, then trod them with their bare feet and dried them in the sun. The dried powder was boiled in water to make chuño, a thick potato soup.

▲ These potatoes are just one of several hundred Andean varieties still grown in South America today.

◀ Potatoes for chuño, drying in the sun in Peru.

In the sixteenth century, Spanish explorers discovered the Inca empire, and took potatoes back to Spain. Monks in Spain began growing potatoes to feed to the sick, and gradually potatoes spread to Italy and the rest of Europe.

At first, potatoes were eaten mainly by poor people or fed to animals. Potatoes come from the same plant family as the poisonous deadly nightshade, which made people think that they might be poisonous. There were also rumours that potatoes caused a disease called leprosy.

In eighteenth-century France, potatoes were made fashionable by the chemist Antoine-Augustin Parmentier, who wrote books praising them and served dinners with potatoes for every course. People wore potato flowers in their buttonholes, Queen Marie Antoinette wore them in her hair and they were embroidered on King Louis XVI's robes.

Legend says that the explorer Sir Francis Drake brought potatoes back to England in 1586 but that cooks at the court of Queen Elizabeth I served the green stems and leaves, which gave everyone stomach ache.

▶ Sir Francis Drake (1545–96).

◀ Antoine-Augustin Parmentier (1737–1813) made potatoes fashionable in eighteenth-century France.

Potatoes in war and peace

For centuries, potatoes were the staple diet of poor people in Ireland because they were cheap and easy to grow. A small plot could feed a family of eight. One story says that Sir Walter Raleigh (1552–1618) took potatoes to Ireland. Another says that they arrived on a wrecked ship from the Spanish Armada, a fleet of ships sent to attack Britain, which was defeated in 1588.

▼ This drawing of 1846 shows a poor Irish widow and her children. During the potato famine, millions of people had to leave their homes and starved to death.

When the British leader, Oliver Cromwell, invaded Ireland in 1649, his soldiers destroyed all the grain crops they could see, but potatoes were safe because they were growing under the ground.

In 1845, a disease called potato blight spread to Ireland. Potatoes rotted in the fields and the harvest was ruined. One million people starved to death. About one million more were forced to emigrate to other countries because they had nothing to eat and could not pay the rent for their homes to their British landlords.

In Victorian Britain, baked potatoes were sold by streetsellers. They were bought to eat, but were useful in warming people's hands on cold nights. Fried fish shops, which were introduced in the nineteenth century, served fish with baked potatoes or bread. In the 1870s, they started serving chips (French fries), which were introduced from France.

▲ A baked potato seller in Victorian London.

During the Second World War (1939–45), food was scarce and millions of tonnes of extra potatoes were planted to help feed the people when other food supplies were rationed. The British Government told people to 'dig for victory' and potatoes were planted in parks, gardens and even on roadside verges.

◀ 'Potato Pete', a character who appeared on posters during the Second World War. He encouraged people to eat more potatoes with his slogan 'I'm an energy food!'

9

What is a potato?

The potato is a member of the nightshade family of plants, called the solanaceae. Nightshades are one of our most important sources of food and medicines. They include tomatoes, aubergines, sweet peppers and petunias, as well as poisonous plants like deadly nightshade and tobacco.

The potato plant has stems, leaves, flowers, fruits and roots. We eat the tubers, lumps which grow on the stems under the ground. These tubers contain starchy carbohydrates which are a food store for potato plants, and provide a nutritious food for us. Other tubers that we eat include Jerusalem artichokes and sweet potatoes. In tropical countries, another kind of tuber called a yam is a very important food.

▲ Potatoes belong to the same family of plants as these colourful petunias.

▶ When potatoes are lifted out of the earth, we can see the roots and tubers which grow under the ground.

Sweet potatoes, which are believed to have been the first potatoes brought back to Europe from South America by the Spanish.

Scientists called plant breeders work to create new kinds of potato by cross-breeding different types of potato plants.

Some types of potato are firm and moist inside. They are usually called waxy potatoes. They have more water and less starch than other types and keep their shape when cooked, so they are good for boiling, steaming and roasting. Others are drier inside and have a higher starch content. They are called floury potatoes, and are best for mashing, baking and deep frying. To decide if a potato is waxy or floury, mix a bowl of two parts water to one part salt. Waxy potatoes will float, but floury potatoes will sink.

Some types of potato are more moist and firm inside than others.

11

How potatoes grow

Potato plants grow from healthy seed potatoes. In the skin of the seed potato are leaf buds called eyes, where shoots start to grow. The shoots grow leaves, using as food the carbohydrate stored in the potato. When this is all used up, the plant starts to make its own food. It sends out lots of roots, covered with tiny hairs which take up water and food from the soil.

▲ The tiny buds on these potatoes are eyes, which produce the shoots.

◀ Earth is piled around potato plants to stop sunlight reaching the tubers, as it can turn them green and bitter.

As the shoot reaches the surface, leaves unfold to catch the light. Plants make energy from sunlight through photosynthesis. Sunlight on the leaves makes chlorophyll, the green colouring in the leaves. Chlorophyll uses carbon dioxide gas from air and hydrogen gas from water to make carbohydrate. Then the seed potato rots and the plant stores the food it makes under ground in the tubers, which are the new potatoes. A potato plant can grow up to twenty tubers. Tubers can grow up to 15 cm long and can weigh up to 1.5 kg.

12

Above ground, the potato plant forms buds and flowers. The flowers may be white, pink or purple. Insects carry pollen from flower to flower, so they are fertilized and make fruits. Potato fruits are round and green, about the size of marbles. They are poisonous, but they contain lots of seeds which could grow into new plants. After about twelve weeks, the potato plant stops growing and the leaves die back. The potatoes are then ready to be harvested by machine or by hand.

▲ This field of potato plants in Italy is just coming into flower.

▼ On this small farm in Spain, potatoes are harvested by hand.

The food in potatoes

Potatoes are nutritious and easy to digest. They are rich in starchy carbohydrates, which are a healthy source of energy. Starchy carbohydrates are found in potatoes, pasta, bread and rice. The body breaks them down into glucose to make energy. One hundred grams of potato provides about the same amount of energy as 40 g of bread.

▼ Crisps are a popular way of eating potatoes all over the world.

▲ Potatoes, like bread, rice and pasta, are healthy sources of energy.

Potatoes contain lots of fibre. We need fibre to help us digest and pass food through our bodies. They also contain a small amount of protein, which we use to grow and repair our bodies.

Some potatoes have soft, thin skins and do not have to be peeled before eating. Potatoes in their skins are very nutritious.

Vitamins and minerals are found just under the skin of potatoes, so it is good to eat them in their skins. Potatoes are especially rich in Vitamin C and 100 g of potato provides about half the Vitamin C a person needs every day. Vitamins and minerals can be lost when potatoes are boiled so steaming is a healthier way of cooking them.

Potatoes can be eaten with fish, poultry, meat, vegetables, cheese and eggs to form part of a balanced diet.

By the end of the eighteenth century, sailors were taking potatoes on long voyages, as a source of Vitamin C. Without enough Vitamin C in their diet, they suffered from diseases like scurvy.

Potatoes can form part of a healthy, balanced meal.

100 grams of raw potato contains:
78.8 grams of water
15.6 grams of starch
2.1 grams of protein
1.7 grams of fibre
1.3 grams of sugar
0.2 grams of fat
7–19 milligrams of Vitamin C
75 kilocalories of energy
small amounts of Vitamins A, B_1 and B_2 and minerals
including calcium, iron, potassium, phosphorus and sodium

15

Potato farming

In spring, farmers give their seed potatoes some light and warmth so that shoots start to grow. Before planting, the farmer ploughs the field and uses a machine to remove stones which could damage the potatoes. The tractor then tows the potato planter which drops the seed potatoes in rows under ridges of soil. It is important that no light gets to the growing tubers or they will turn green and taste bitter.

▲ This man in China is weeding his crop of potatoes by hand.

Early potatoes are planted from January onwards and harvested in the summer. The farmer may need to protect them from frost in the winter months by covering the rows with plastic sheeting. Main crop potatoes are planted in March or April and are ready to be harvested in August or September.

Potatoes need food, water and sunshine to grow. The farmer may use animal manure or fertilizer to feed the soil. Potatoes can be attacked by pests like snails and slugs and by fungi and disease. Some farmers use chemical sprays to protect the crop. Organic farmers do not use chemicals because they believe that they are harmful to people and the environment.

◀ In dry weather, potatoes need to be watered to help them grow.

This farmer in the USA tends his potato crop.

Potatoes are harvested by a machine which lifts the plants out of the ground and shakes off the soil and any stones. Farm workers take out any damaged or green potatoes and the good ones fall into a trailer to be taken back to the farm.

Potatoes must be stored in the semi-dark in a cool, dry shed to stop them from sprouting or freezing. They are sorted into sizes, then washed and packed to be sold or processed.

Potatoes are harvested using a mechanical harvester.

17

Processing potatoes

▲ Potatoes being sorted into different sizes at a farm in the UK. They will then be sold for processing.

More than half of the potatoes we eat are prepared as processed foods. This means that they are treated in some way, to make them easier to store and cook. Potato processing began in the First World War (1914–18) to supply army food stores.

Today, potato processing factories have machines which prepare and cook the potatoes. They are used in products like chips, crisps, potato waffles, pancakes, croquettes and toppings for pies. New potatoes can be peeled and canned in salted water, ready for use. Chopped potatoes are used in soups, stews and packs of mixed vegetables. They are also cooked and dried as flakes or powder, which can be mixed with milk or water to make quick mashed potato.

► These factory workers are checking potato chips as they pass along a moving belt.

◀ Crisps are one of the most popular processed potato foods in the world. Healthier crisps are now made, containing less fat and salt.

▼ Croquette potatoes are sold chilled or frozen, ready to heat and serve.

To make chips and crisps, factories use special machines to clean, peel and wash the potatoes. They are then sliced and part-cooked before being deep fried in oil. Crisps are sprayed with salt and flavourings and packaged in airtight bags. It takes five tonnes of raw potatoes to make one tonne of crisps. Chips may be dried in hot air to give them a crisp coating so that they are ready to bake in the oven at home.

The starch from potatoes is used in some drinks, sweets and cracker biscuits. Potatoes can also be used to make alcoholic drinks, including Russian vodka, Scandinavian aquavit and a Peruvian beer called chicha. Damaged or sprouting potatoes may be used to make animal feed for cows and pigs.

Cooking potatoes

Potatoes cannot be eaten raw, as some vegetables can, but there are lots of different ways of cooking them. Raw potatoes are hard and become softer as they cook. The cells which make up a potato contain grains of starch which swell and stick together as the potato cooks.

Potatoes can be boiled in water, steamed, fried or baked in the oven. Baking is a healthy way to cook potatoes and it is good to eat the nutritious skins. Steaming or microwaving also keeps in the goodness. Frying potatoes is the best way of keeping Vitamin C, but increases the fat. We should try not to eat too many fatty fried foods as too much fat in our diet can lead to heart disease. Oven chips are healthier as they need no extra fat to be cooked.

▲ Boiled potatoes can be served mashed and are low in fat. However, fat is found in the milk and butter added to mashed potato.

Potatoes should not be eaten when they are green. Green patches are a substance called solanine, which is bitter and can be poisonous.

▶ Potatoes can be roasted in fat in the oven, but it is more healthy to use little or no fat.

20

◀ Mashed potato makes a tasty topping for fish or meat dishes like this.

▼ Rösti is a golden potato cake from Switzerland. It is made by frying grated potato, and is sometimes flavoured with chopped onion or bacon.

Boiled potatoes can be mashed, then shaped into fingers covered in a crispy coating of egg and breadcrumbs and fried to make croquettes.

Grated potatoes can be made into a fried potato cake called rösti, or mixed into dough for making pastry, bread or scones. Potato pancakes can be made by mixing grated potato with eggs, milk and butter. Chopped or mashed potato can be used in soups, stews and meat or vegetable loaves and as a topping for savoury pies.

Potato customs and beliefs

In the Inca empire of South America, the potato was considered a gift from the gods, and was praised and honoured in special ceremonies. The Incas had over 1,000 different names for the potato, and even measured time in units of 'how long it takes to cook a potato'.

▲ Potatoes have been grown on this land near Cuzco, Peru since the time of the Incas. Inca ruins can be seen nearby.

There are lots of superstitions based on potatoes, some dating back for centuries. Some peoples believed that potatoes should only be planted 'in the dark of the moon' and Russian peasants buried balls of amber in their fields to protect the potato plants from disease.

Potatoes have been thought of as a medicine, and were used to cure problems from gout and frostbite to warts and burns. Potatoes were also believed to have special cleaning powers. Raw potato was used to clean paintings, and the water in which potatoes had been boiled was used to make cutlery or silver sparkle.

◄ This drawing of a type of potato plant appeared in a book in 1796.

22

Carrying a raw potato in your pocket all year was said to cure toothache and stop you catching cold and 'flu, because the potato caught them instead. In Poland, potatoes were dressed with moss and twigs and used as talismans to cast spells or get rid of evil spirits.

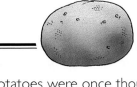

Potatoes were once thought of as medicine. King Philip II of Spain (1556–98) sent potatoes to the Pope as a cure for gout.

▼ This painting by the nineteenth-century French artist JF Millet shows peasants praying to give thanks for the potato harvest.

▶ King Philip II of Spain (1527–98).

Potato dishes from around the world

Bubble and squeak is a traditional British dish of left-over mashed potatoes and cabbage or other vegetables. The dish is fried in hot oil and probably gets its name from the sizzling sound it makes as it cooks.

The Scandinavians cook sugar-browned potatoes as a Christmas treat. In Britain, roast potatoes are an important part of the traditional Christmas dinner.

Duchess potatoes, a French dish, is made with mashed potato, which is piped into circles and baked in the oven until golden.

The Germans cook a dish called Heaven and Earth, made from frankfurters or bacon cooked with potatoes (from the earth) and apples (from the heavens).

▲ Jewish latkes are fried cakes of grated potato with egg, flour and sugar.

◀ Gnocchi are Italian potato dumplings. Mashed potato is mixed into dough with egg and flour, then shaped and boiled in water.

Crisps are called potato chips in the USA. There is a story that crisps were invented in New York, USA, in 1853, after a customer in a restaurant complained about his thick fried potatoes. The chef went back into the kitchen, cut extra thin slices of potato and fried them.

24

Potatoes are cooked with mutton or lamb for an Irish stew.

Potatoes boulangère is a French dish of baked, sliced potatoes and onions in stock. This dish takes its name from French bakeries (boulangeries) because villagers used to take the dish to the bakery to be cooked in the bread ovens, saving them the cost of fuel.

Chips are a popular fast food all over the world. The Belgians eat chips with plates of steaming hot mussels while, in France, steak and chips (steak-frites) is popular.

Onions are added to potatoes to make hash browns, which are popular in the USA.

▲ Potatoes Dauphinoise is a French dish of thinly sliced potato, baked in the oven with milk or cream. Garlic and nutmeg may be used to add flavour.

In Mexico, potatoes are sometimes cut into matchsticks and deep fried in batter with chopped chillies and chillie powder.

In Iran, potatoes may be baked in the oven with grated turnip, in milk and cinnamon.

Indian cooks sometimes prepare potatoes by cutting them into cubes and boiling them, then frying them with some cumin and sesame seeds, a little black mustard, cayenne pepper, salt and lemon juice.

▲ Hungarian goulash is a rich stew made from beef, potatoes and onions.

Potato recipes for you to try

Baked potato surprises

To serve four people you will need:

4 baking potatoes
50 g cheddar cheese
25 g butter
4 eggs
salt and pepper

1 Bake the potatoes in an oven at 200° Centigrade (400° Fahrenheit, gas mark 6) for about one to one and a half hours, until they feel soft when you squeeze them.

2 Ask an adult to help you to cut a 'lid' from the top of each potato. Scoop out the flesh and mash it with the butter and a pinch of salt and pepper.

3 Spoon half of the potato back into the skins, and make a nest in each with the back of a spoon.

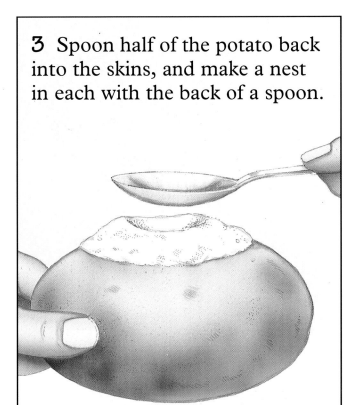

4 Carefully break an egg into each potato. Sprinkle with the grated cheese and arrange the potatoes with their lids on in an ovenproof dish. Bake for another fifteen minutes in the oven until the eggs have set.

Serve with crusty bread or a salad.

Potato pie

To serve four people you will need:

1½ kg potatoes
250 g cooked ham, chopped
1 onion, chopped
500 ml soured cream
2 tablespoons breadcrumbs
100 g cheddar cheese, grated
1 egg
50 g butter
salt and pepper

1 Peel the potatoes. Ask an adult to help you to heat a large saucepan of water. Cook the potatoes with a pinch of salt for twenty-five to thirty minutes, or until they are soft.

2 Heat the oven to 200° Centigrade (400° Fahrenheit, gas mark 6). Drain the potatoes. When they are cool, ask an adult to help you to cut them into slices.

3 Arrange about half of the potato slices in the bottom of a greased ovenproof dish. Sprinkle over the chopped ham and onion, then make another layer of the rest of the potatoes.

4 In a separate bowl, mix together the soured cream and egg with a pinch of salt and pepper. Carefully pour this over the potatoes.

5 Sprinkle the breadcrumbs and grated cheese over the top and add a few small pieces of butter. Bake in the oven for about forty minutes.

Serve hot with a salad or green vegetables.

29

Glossary

airtight Sealed so that no air can enter or escape.

amber A hard, clear orange substance, sometimes used to make jewellery.

Armada A fleet of Spanish warships that attacked Britain in 1588.

calories Short for kilocalories, measurements of the energy in food.

carbohydrates A kind of food including sugars and starches which we need to keep us warm and give us energy.

chlorophyll A substance in plants that makes the leaves green.

cholesterol A type of fat found in the body and in food. Too much cholesterol can cause heart disease.

croquettes Small pieces of food that have been shaped into rolls, coated with breadcrumbs and fried.

cross-breeding Breeding two different types of the same animal or plant.

emigrate To leave the country where you live and to move to a new country.

empire Land or countries under the power of one ruler or government.

environment The natural world, including the landscape, plants, humans and animals.

eyes Scars on potato from which shoots grow.

fertilized Female cells that have been combined with male cells to create new life.

fertilizer A substance that is added to soil to provide food for plants.

fibre The part of food which helps us to digest food and pass it through our bodies.

fungi A type of plant. Some types of fungi can harm other plants or animals.

glucose A type of sugar found in starch.

gout A disease which causes body joints to swell.

Kilocalories A measurement of the energy-producing value in food.

leprosy A disease that affects the skin and nerves.

nutritious Containing substances that we need to keep us healthy.

manure Animal dung, which is sometimes used to fertilize the soil.

minerals Substances found in food that we need to keep our bodies healthy.

organic farmers Farmers who use natural farming methods without chemicals.

photosynthesis The process by which green plants make food, using sunlight.

pollen Powdery grains from flowers which carry the male cells to the female parts of the flower, causing fertilization.

processed foods Foods that have been prepared for easier storage and cooking.

protein A substance found in food that we need to grow and repair our bodies.

rationed Limited amounts.

scurvy A disease caused by lack of Vitamin C.

seed potatoes Potatoes that are sown in the ground and which grow into new plants.

slogan A catchy phrase used in advertising.

smallholdings Small farms.

Solanaceae The family of plants from which potatoes come.

solanine A bitter substance found in potatoes that makes them go green.

starch A kind of carbohydrate found in cereals and potatoes.

stock A liquid made from water and vegetable, fish or meat juices.

superstitions Beliefs that cannot be scientifically proved.

talismans Objects that are believed to have magic power and to bring good luck.

tropical Having a hot, wet climate.

tubers Underground swellings on the stem of a plant.

verges Strips of grass along the edges of roads.

Victorian The period in British history when Queen Victoria was Queen (1837–1901).

vitamins Substances found in food that we need to keep us healthy.

waffles Thick, fried pancakes made from batter or grated potato.

Books to read

Food in History by Sheila Robertson (Wayland, 1993)

Potatoes by Joy Palmer (Hodder and Stoughton, 1989)

Potatoes by Dorothy Turner (Wayland, 1988)

The Story of the Potato by Alan Wilson (Balding and Mansell, 1993)

For further information about potatoes, contact:

The Potato Marketing Board, Broad Field House, 4 Between Towns Road, Cowley, Oxford OX4 3NA.

Index